A Fruit and Vegetable Education

By Michael Reed

Copyright © 2013 by MR

Acknowledgements

I want to thank God and others for the idea and materials for the book.

Apples, grapes, and oranges are some of the fruits that you enjoy on Earth. However, some vegetables such as tomatoes and chili peppers are fruits because they are produced by flowers on their plants.

06/02/13

Ferns, pines, and mosses are among some of the plant kinds that do not produce fruits because they do not have flowers with enclosed seeds. Like flowering plants, they reproduce after their kinds.

Ferns and mosses reproduce through spores that are located in special containers and capsules. A female pine cone does not have an enclosed ovary like a flowering plant, and their seeds are formed on the scales of the female cones. However, it receives pollen from the smaller male cone.

1. Moss clump

2. Fern frond

3. Female pine cone

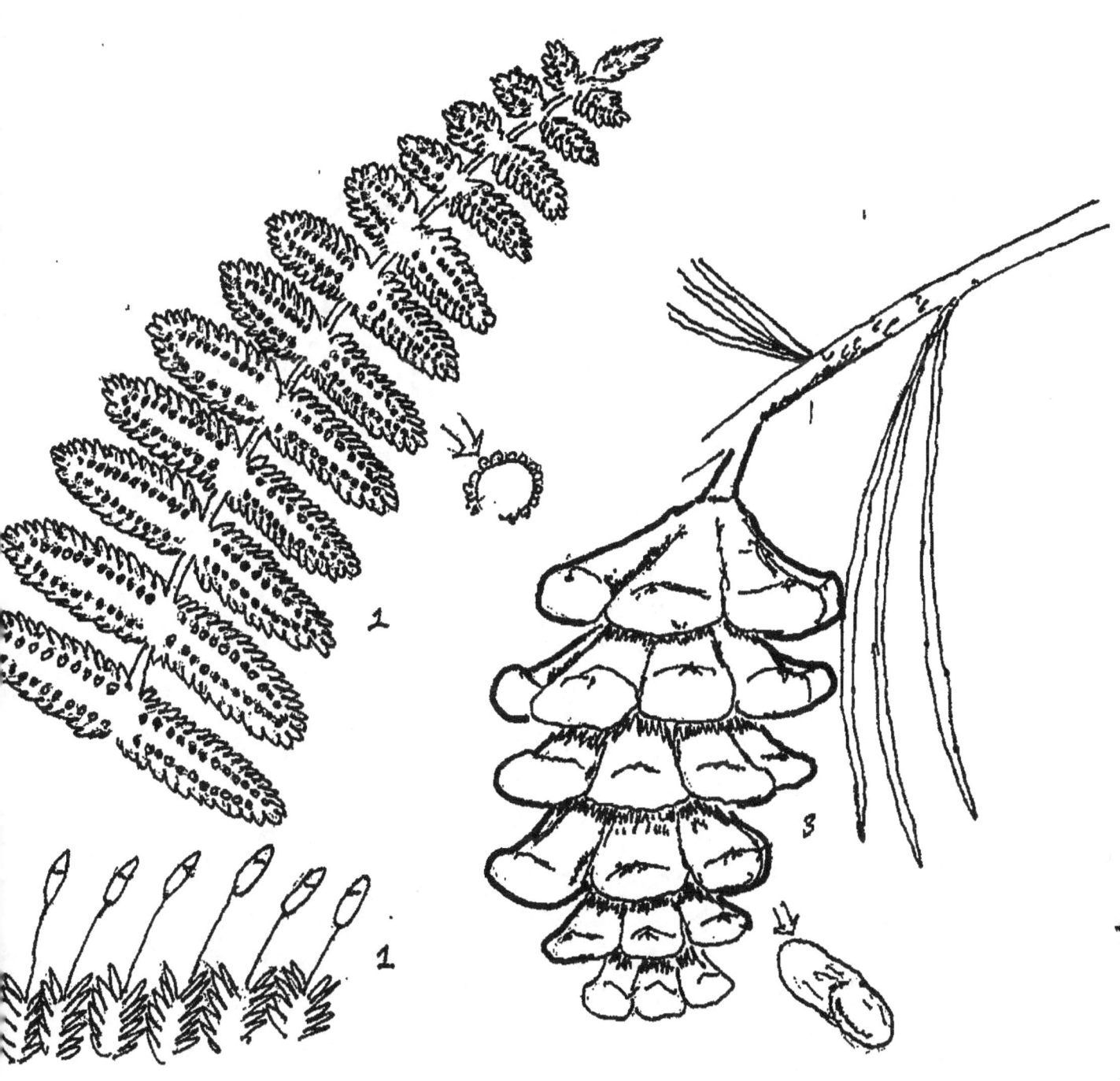

1

3

1

3

06/04/13

Do you know how fruits are made?

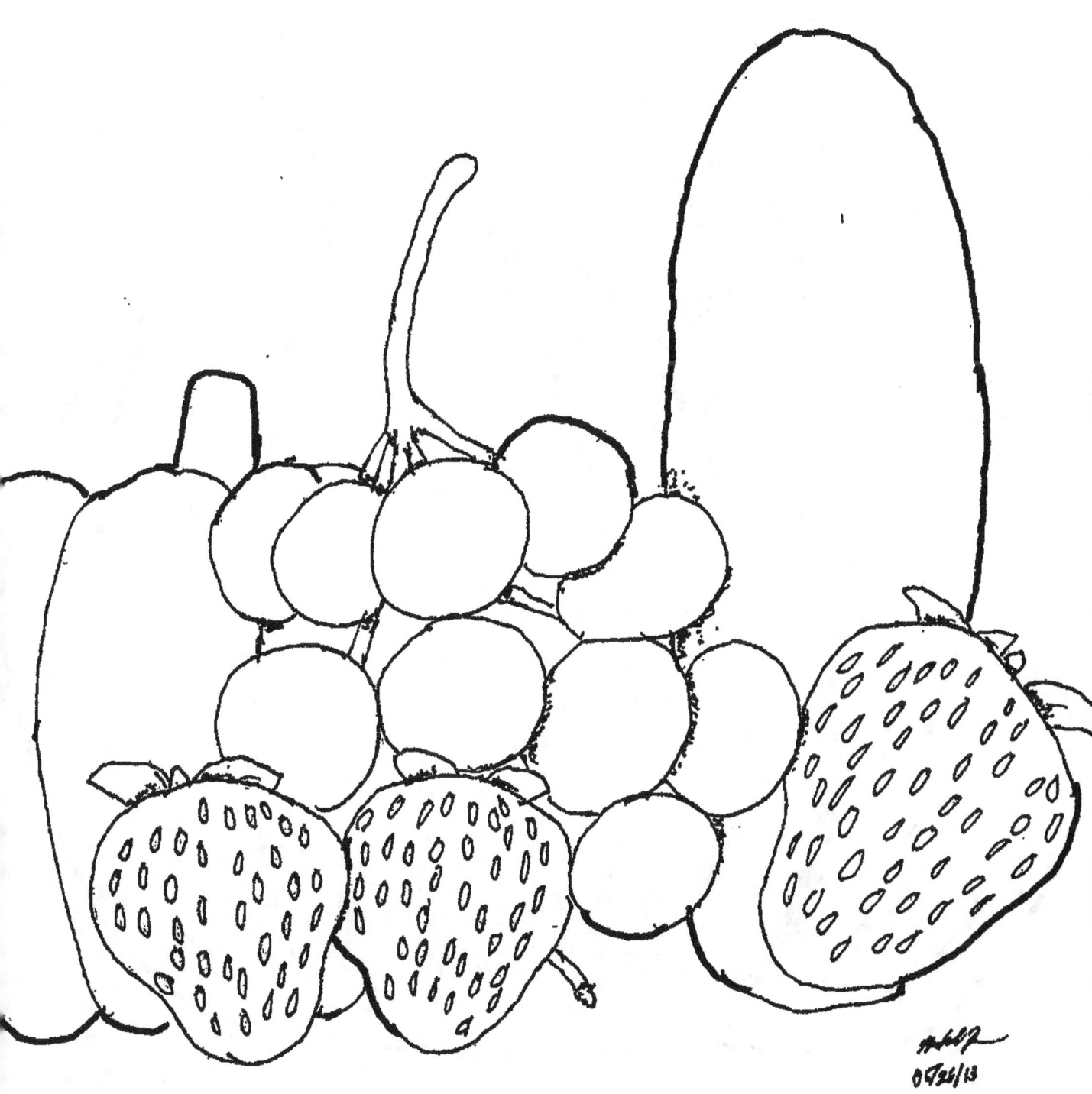

Fruits are formed when the pollen grains land on the pistil. The grains are formed on the stamen, the male part of the flower. Soon, they are transferred to the top of the pistil by either an animal or the wind.

The following steps of this example can help to explain it.

1. The pollen is produce in the anther, the top structure of the stamen of the flower.

2. The bee helps to transfer the pollen grains to another flower.

3. The pollen grains land on the pistil. Biological and chemical changes help to transform the pistil into a fruit.

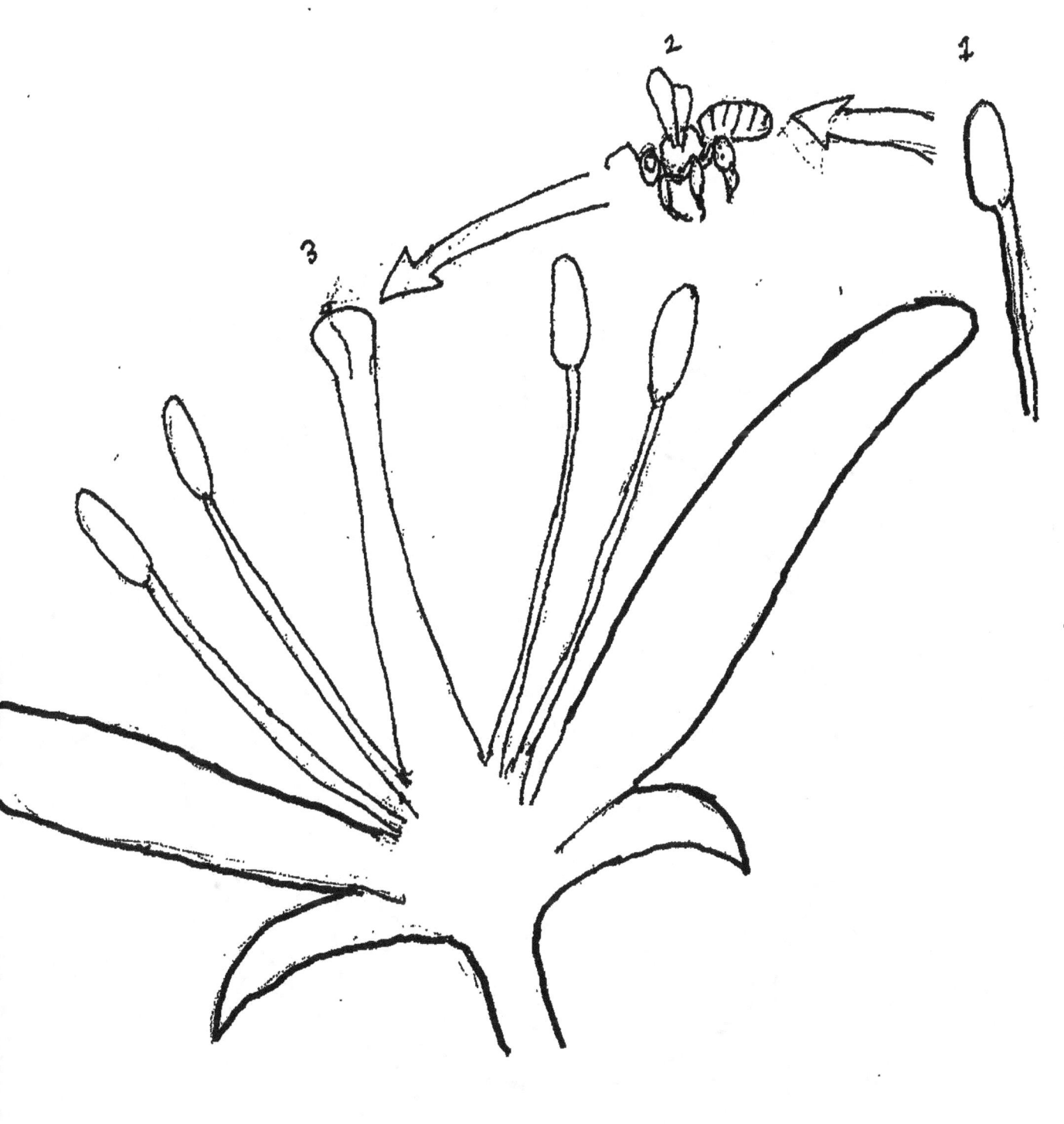

Flowering plants are made in various designs, from the smallest flower to the largest tree.

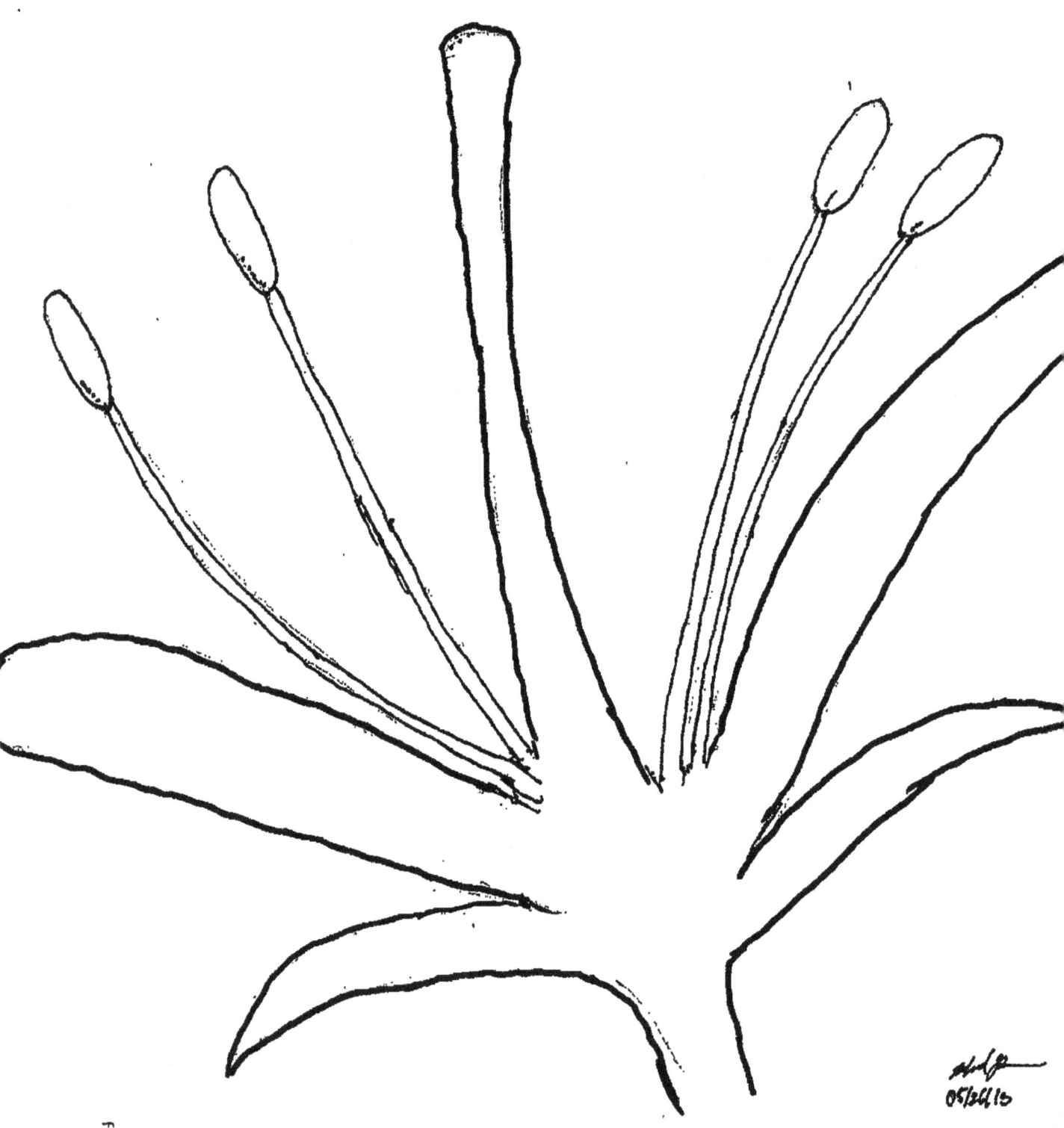

There are many kinds of flowering plants that produce fruits. Botanists, people who study plants, help to classify them into families by their characteristics.

In your grocery store, there are some fruits that are labeled as vegetables. In this section, there are some examples of fruits and vegetables in the following pages.

Cucumbers, squashes, and the watermelon are fruits that are classified in the Gourd Family (Cucurbitaceae), while the apples, cherries, and peaches are grouped in the Rose Family (Rosaceae).

1. Cucumbers   4. Apples

2. Squashes   5. Peaches

3. Watermelon   6. Cherries

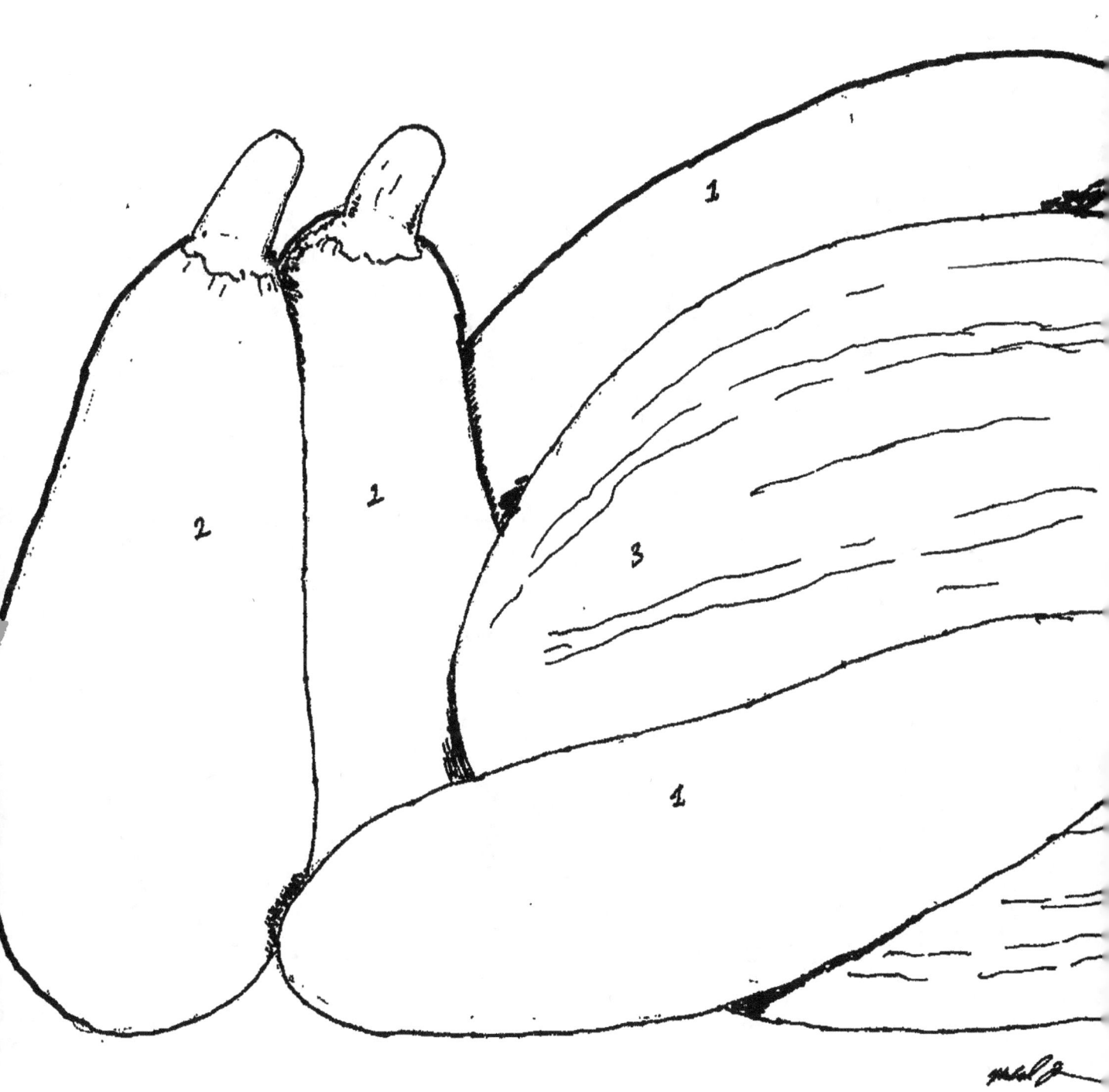

Our sunflowers seeds are produced from the plant that is classified in the Sunflower Family (Compositae). The materials for the bread, rice grains, and popcorn seeds are produced from their plants, which are in the Grass Family (Poaceae).

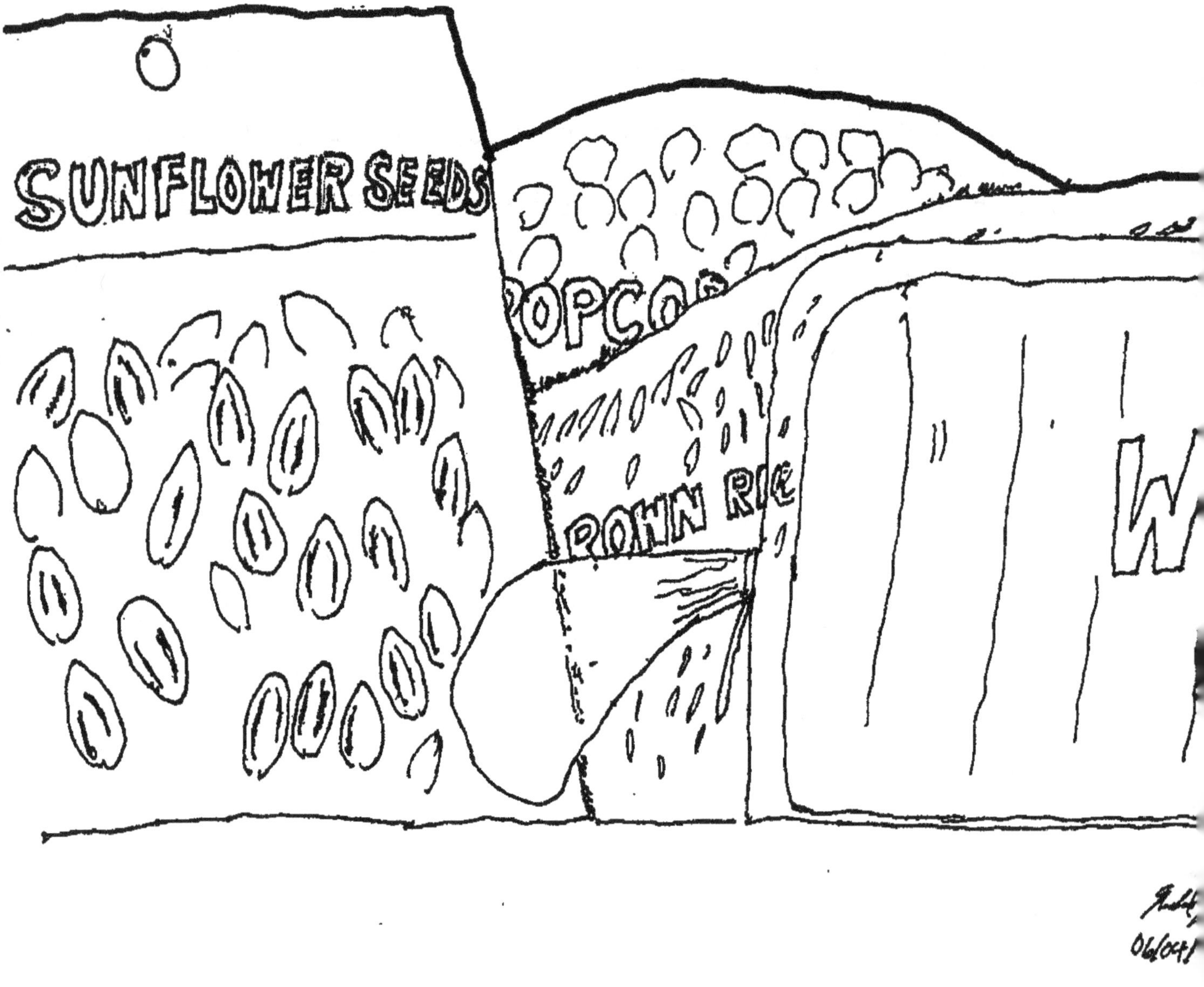
SUNFLOWER SEEDS
POPCOR
ROHN RIC

Onion and garlic bulbs are not fruits, because they are structures that are surrounded by leaves with a flattened root. Nevertheless, they are an important part of our produce because of their uses for food and other needs. These bulbs come from plants that are classified in the Lily Family (Liliaceae).

Tomatoes, bell and chili peppers are produced by plants that are grouped in the Potato Family (Solanaceae).

1. Onions
2. Garlic bulbs
3. Tomatoes
4. Bell Peppers
5. Chili Peppers

Oranges, lemons, and grape fruits are classified in the Citrus (Rutaceae) Family, while the grapes are classified in the family Vitaceae.

1. Oranges

2. Lemons

3. Grapefruits

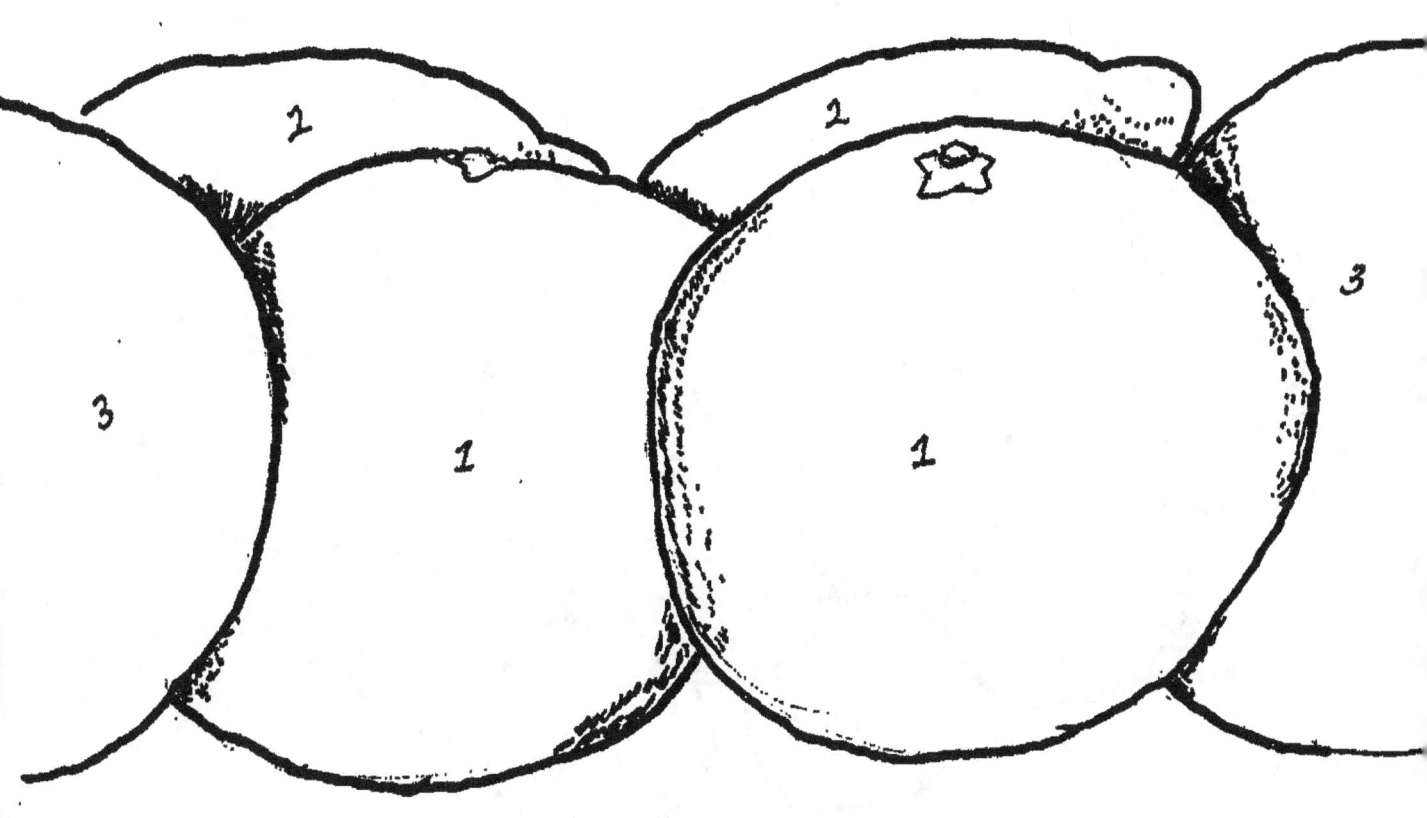

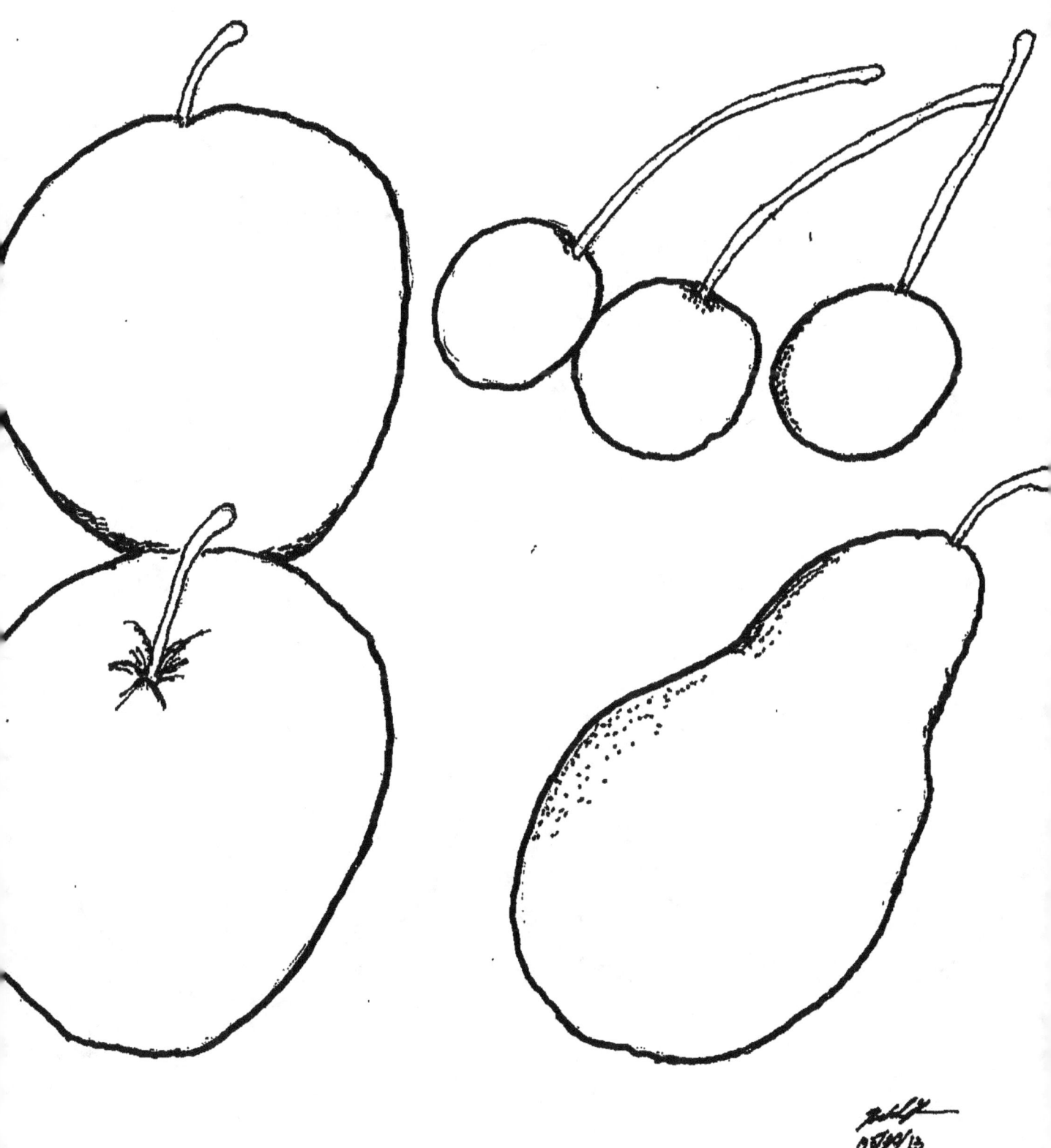

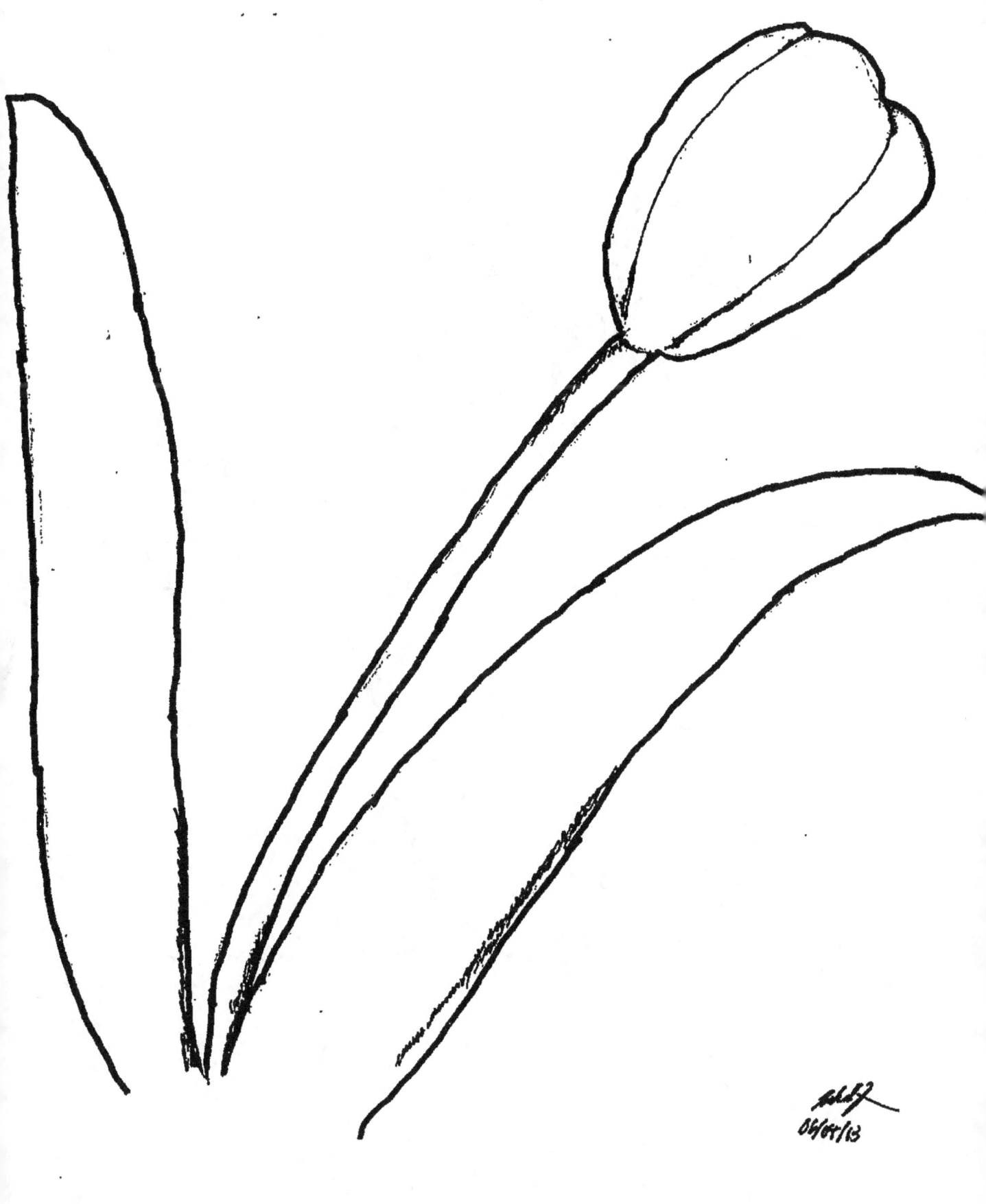

You can learn and read more about the science of fruits and vegetables in places such as schools, libraries, and natural history and/or science museums. Also, you can use books and computers for references for further produce research.

Some Materials for Research

Burnie, David. Eyewitness Books: Plant. Alfred A Knopf: New York. 1989.

Cavendish, Marshall and Barbara Taylor. Invisible Worlds: Inside Plants. Benchmark, New York. 2011.

Heywood, Prof V.H et al. Flowering Plants of the World. Oxford University Press, New York. 1993.

Levine Shar and Leslie Johnstone. A Class of their Own: Plants, Flowering Plants, Ferns,Mosses, and Other Plants. Crabtree Publishing Company, New York. 2010.

Silverthorne, Elizabeth. Real World Science: Plants. Cherry Lake Publishing, Ann Arbor. 2009.

www.ingramcontent.com/pod-product-compliance
Lightning Source LLC
Chambersburg PA
CBHW081134280526

45787CB00007B/3072